A History of Germs

SMALLPOX

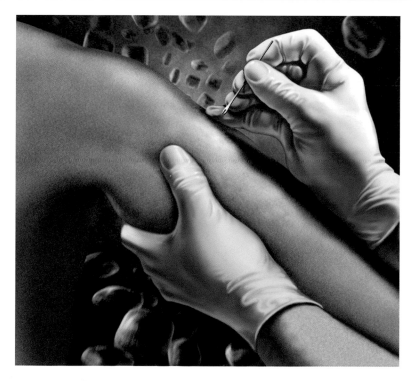

 By Jim Ollhoff

Editor: John Hamilton
Graphic Design: Sue Hamilton
Cover Design: John Hamilton
Cover Photo: Getty Images
Interior Photos and Illustrations: Centers for Disease Control and Prevention-Pg 31; Corbis-pgs 14, 22, 24, 27, 28, & 29; Getty Images-pgs 1, 9, 12, 15, 19 & 20; The Granger Collection-pgs 7, 8, 13, & 18; iStockphoto-pg 3; Jupiterimages-pg 16; North Wind Picture Archives-pg 17; Photo Researchers-pgs 4, 5, 10, 11, & 23.

Library of Congress Cataloging-in-Publication Data

Ollhoff, Jim, 1959-
  Smallpox / Jim Ollhoff.
      p. cm. – (A history of germs)
  Includes index.
  ISBN 978-1-60453-501-3
  1. Smallpox–Juvenile literature. I. Title.

 QR201.S6O45 2010
 616.9'12–dc22

                                    2008055060

CONTENTS

HISTORY'S KILLER

One of the deadliest killers the world has ever known sits in a cell in Atlanta, Georgia. This killer is under heavy guard, awaiting execution. The killer is the smallpox virus. It is responsible for millions of deaths throughout history. Smallpox was fatal for about 30 percent of the people who became infected.

Worldwide vaccinations have wiped smallpox from the face of the earth.

A transmission electron micrograph (TEM) of smallpox viruses.

People who got smallpox had tiny little bumps all over their bodies. Pox is from the Latin word for "spotted," referring to the raised bumps. The scientific name of the virus is *Variola*.

But, in one of the greatest victories in the history of medicine, the disease has been eradicated. This means that it is no longer in nature—it cannot infect people anymore. Aggressive vaccinations in the 1960s and 1970s wiped it off the earth.

Today, only a small amount of the virus exists—well contained at the Centers for Disease Control and Prevention in Atlanta, Georgia, and at a similar laboratory in Russia. Some scientists say the remaining virus should be destroyed so it can never escape into the world again. Other scientists say it should be preserved so that it can be studied, and help us better prepare for the next dangerous virus that comes along.

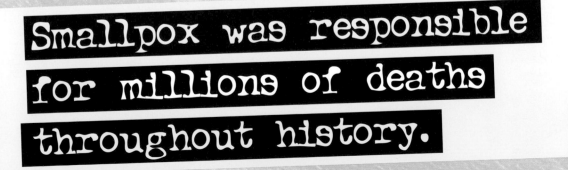

Smallpox was responsible for millions of deaths throughout history.

A BRIEF HISTORY OF SMALLPOX

The smallpox virus emerged long before recorded civilization. DNA analysis suggests that it became dangerous to humans at least 16,000 years ago, and probably much sooner.

History is often cloudy about smallpox epidemics. When describing plagues, ancient doctors did not use the kind of diagnostic language we use today. It is difficult to know if they were describing smallpox or something else. Sometimes, ancient doctors wrote about "the pox," but that could refer to any number of diseases that created eruptions on the skin. Sometimes doctors said people died of an "acute illness," but weren't specific about what kind of illness.

The first person that scientists know of who had smallpox was Ramses V, the Pharaoh of Egypt, who died about 1157 BC. When archeologists first unwrapped his mummified body, his skin had the familiar bumps and pockmarks of smallpox.

Ramses V's pockmarked face is shown on a museum wall display and at left. It is believed that he died of smallpox.

Historians think smallpox reached India about 1000 BC. In China, doctors described a smallpox-like plague in 1122 BC. Smallpox was probably the source of the great plague of Athens, Greece, in 430 BC. Smallpox was also the likely cause of the Roman plague of Antonine, which lasted through the years 165 to 180 AD, and killed almost seven million people.

Waves of smallpox epidemics occurred in the Middle East, North Africa, and Europe throughout the Middle Ages. Persian physicians described smallpox in a medical paper in 910 AD. It wasn't until the 1500s that European doctors began to refer to the disease as "the small pox," to distinguish it from the larger pox of other skin eruptions. Historians estimate that during the 1700s, smallpox killed nearly one-half-million Europeans every year.

A young Chinese girl is shown in a painting suffering from smallpox.

An illustration shows Aztec victims of the 1538 smallpox epidemic covered with shrouds (center), as two other natives covered in pox are about to die (right).

Beginning in 1520, Spanish conquistador Hernán Cortéz invaded Central America. Some of his men were carriers of smallpox, and they infected the Aztecs and other native populations. Many of the Spaniards were immune to the smallpox virus, but the native population of Central America had no such immunity. Having never been exposed to smallpox before, the virus spread like lightning through the people. Historians estimate that 3.5 million Aztec Indians died from the disease. Millions of other native peoples in Central and South America died within a few years.

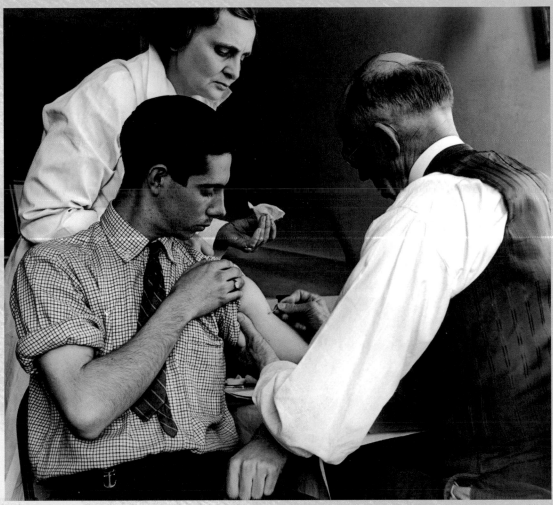

In the late 1960s and 1970s aggressive vaccination programs were conducted around the world. The last natural case of smallpox was in 1977.

In North America, a similar thing happened. European settlers came to North America and unknowingly brought the virus with them. Native American tribes were decimated by smallpox.

The first effective smallpox vaccine was developed in 1796. In the decades after that, smallpox rates declined in more developed countries. But even as late as the 1950s, millions of people across the world died from smallpox. Aggressive vaccination programs went on in the late 1960s and 1970s. The last natural case of smallpox was in 1977.

INFECTION AND SYMPTOMS

Smallpox is a virus, a small bundle of DNA. Bacteria and viruses are different kinds of germs. Bacteria are living cells, but viruses are not. Viruses get into a body and then inject their DNA into a normal cell. The virus hijacks the cell, tricking the cell into producing more viruses.

The smallpox virus comes in two types: the deadly *Variola major*, and a less dangerous virus called *Variola minor*. About 30 percent of those who contracted *Variola major* died.

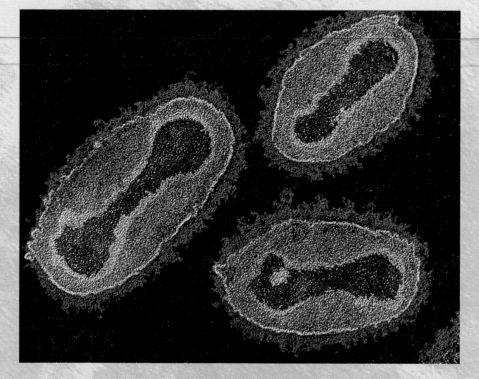

Color enhanced transmission electron microscope (TEM) image of three smallpox (*Variola major*) viruses.

A simulation of a doctor taking a pus sample from a sore on a person infected with smallpox.

The smallpox virus spreads when a person has direct contact with infected bodily fluids. When tiny droplets of infected pus get into another person's mouth or nose, they can contract the disease. Sometimes, the fluids from a pustule get on clothing or blankets. If another person touches this fluid, and then touches their own nose, the virus can get into their body. In rare cases, tiny droplets of infected fluid float through the air and are inhaled by another person. The virus is highly contagious, but typically only through person-to-person contact.

Once inside the body, the smallpox virus lodges in the soft, wet tissues of the nose, mouth, or throat. From there, it silently reproduces for about 12 days. Then, the infected person begins to feel symptoms resembling a bad cold—fever, muscle pain, headache, and vomiting. After two to four more days, small red spots begin to appear on the mouth, tongue, and throat. A day or two after that, red pustules begin to appear on the skin. These pustules begin to fill with fluid. If the person survives, the pustules scab over, and eventually become scars. Smallpox victims who survived the disease had massive scarring on their bodies, and sometimes were also left blind.

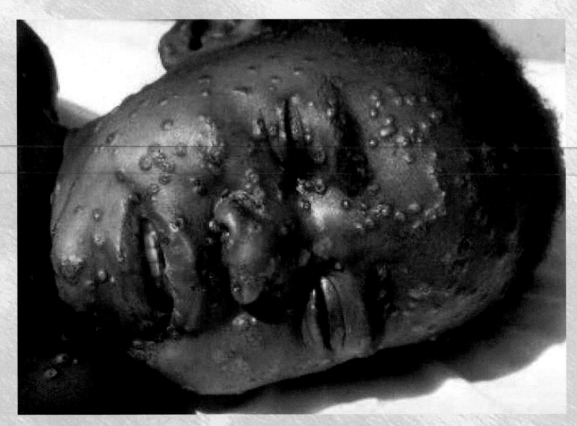

The smallpox virus was spread when a person had direct contact with infected bodily fluids.

Smallpox as a Weapon.

In the past, people sometimes attempted to use smallpox as a weapon. In 1763, the British were fighting a battle with the Ottawa Native Americans of Pennsylvania. The general ordered blankets that had been contaminated with

Native American victims of a smallpox epidemic spread by European settlers in America.

smallpox scabs to be delivered to the Indian tribe. Historians still debate whether the blankets had their intended effect.

In the 1800s, students at medical schools learned anatomy by operating on corpses. However, there was a shortage of corpses for the students. Medical schools often paid unscrupulous people to go out at night and dig up the graves of the recently deceased. In the 1860s, medical students at a school in Cincinnati, Ohio, were particularly mean to a grave robber, playing tricks on him and treating him poorly. The vengeful grave robber dug up and delivered a smallpox victim. Several of the medical students contracted smallpox.

EARLY TREATMENTS

People in early times did not understand bacteria or viruses. It was not until the 1800s that bacteria were identified as the cause of some diseases. Viruses, which couldn't be seen by early microscopes, weren't even discovered until the 1890s.

However, early doctors realized that people who survived smallpox were then immune to the disease. As early as 430 BC, smallpox survivors were called in to help those suffering with the disease.

Doctors began experimenting with ways to give smallpox immunity to others. Ancient Chinese doctors ground up smallpox scabs into a dry powder and had people inhale it. Ancient Persian doctors swallowed smallpox scab powder.

A woman with smallpox lesions. Dried and ground, scabs were once experimentally used as a way to build up immunity to the virus.

A doctor performs a variolation. Fluid from an infected person's smallpox pustule was inserted into a small incision in a healthy person's skin.

In the 1600s in Turkey, doctors made a tiny incision in a healthy person's skin, and then inserted fluid from an infected person's smallpox pustule. This practice became popular in England in the 1700s. It was called *variolation*. It worked most of the time—the person contracted a mild case of smallpox, but the person's immune system was able to fight off the disease. About three percent of the time, however, people who were variolated ended up with a fatal case of smallpox. Even at this rate of fatality, it was better than contracting natural smallpox, which had a 30 percent fatality rate. The practice of variolation grew in Western Europe and the United States during the 1700s.

In 1757, an eight-year-old boy was variolated in England, along with all his classmates. Like most children, he developed a mild case of smallpox and then recovered. His name was Edward Jenner. His thinking about smallpox would later change the world.

Librarian Discovers Smallpox Vaccination Scabs

In March 2003, in a library in Santa Fe, New Mexico, librarian Susanne Caro opened a dusty old book. The book was printed in 1875. It was owned by W.D. Kelly, a surgeon during the Civil War. In the book was an envelope, and on it was written a note that said, "Scabs from vaccination of W.B. Yarrington's children."

Caro knew that smallpox was the only disease that was vaccinated at that time. The question was, were they actually human smallpox scabs? Or were they scabs from cowpox, a mild disease that sometimes gave people immunity to smallpox?

In March 2003, a librarian discovered an envelope in an old book that she thought might contain smallpox scabs. The FBI and the CDC were given the envelope to study the contents. Unfortunately, the DNA had degraded.

Patients are vaccinated against smallpox with a live cowpox virus from a calf.

Caro did some quick research. She learned that by 1875, doctors were using only cowpox to vaccinate people, instead of the much more dangerous human smallpox. The FBI sent the scabs to the Centers for Disease Control and Prevention (CDC) in Atlanta, Georgia. Caro worked with the CDC to find the source of the scabs. She traced it to a time when a woman got smallpox in Galveston, Texas, in 1883. The CDC studied the scabs, hoping to find DNA. This would give scientists a better understanding of how germs change over time. Unfortunately, the wet climate of Galveston had degraded the DNA.

EDWARD JENNER AND THE VACCINE

E dward Jenner was born on May 17, 1749, in the village of Berkeley in the southwestern part of England. Orphaned at age five, he went to live with his older brother. He developed a curiosity about many different things. When he was 13, he went to work for a doctor. During this time, he heard women farmhands say that they had contracted a disease called cowpox. The women claimed they were now immune to the deadlier smallpox disease.

Cowpox was a disease of dairy cows, with small pustules appearing on the cow. It occasionally spread to the hands of farm workers. Doctors of the time dismissed the idea that cowpox prevented smallpox as a silly superstition. But the idea stuck with Edward Jenner.

Jenner collected cowpox vesicles from the hand of a dairymaid, to use for his first vaccination.

Edward Jenner

Jenner became interested in many areas of science. He studied bird migrations, hydrogen-filled balloons, animal hibernation, and the behavior of cuckoo birds. When he was 21, he began an apprenticeship with a well-respected surgeon, Dr. John Hunter. Jenner became a physician himself, and went back to his hometown to practice medicine. He continued to practice a wide variety of scientific hobbies, as well as writing poetry and performing music.

In 1796, Jenner came back to the idea that cowpox could prevent smallpox. Jenner may have been aware of other people who experimented with the cowpox idea. In Jenner's medical practice, he came across a woman who had cowpox. He took fluid from one of her pustules and used it to inoculate an eight-year-old boy named James Phipps. Several days later, the boy developed a mild fever, but otherwise was fine. Then, a few months later, Jenner variolated the boy with smallpox (the common practice of the time). If Phipps were like everyone else, he would contract a mild case of smallpox. However, Phipps remained smallpox-free. The cowpox inoculation worked! Jenner called his process vaccination (vaca means "cow" in Latin).

Jenner gives James Phipps, an eight-year-old boy, the first smallpox inoculation.

Through his vaccinations, Jenner saved millions of lives.

Cowpox inoculation worked because the body's immune system successfully fought off the weak cowpox virus. The smallpox virus and the cowpox virus are similar germs. So, when the smallpox virus attacked the body, the immune system remembered how to fight the cowpox virus, and it easily defeated the smallpox germ.

Jenner wrote up his findings and submitted them to the Royal Society, which was the custom of the time. The society rejected his paper, not believing that the vaccination worked.

Jenner continued his experiments. He wrote a longer paper, with more cases and more information. This time, the Royal Society published Jenner's paper. It had a mixed reception among doctors. Some believed Jenner, others did not.

But, as more and more doctors tried the procedure, the results were indisputable. Jenner gave away his vaccine to whoever asked for it. In the United States, President Thomas Jefferson set up a National Vaccine Institute, which was responsible for getting all Americans vaccinated.

In 1823, at the age of 72, Jenner suffered a fatal stroke. He endured years of ridicule by people who thought he was wrong. But through his vaccinations, he saved millions of lives. His hope was that smallpox would be wiped off the face of the earth. However, that would not happen for 150 years.

ERADICATION OF THE SMALLPOX SCOURGE

Smallpox deaths dropped quickly in the countries that used the vaccine. Western Europe and the United States were rich enough to afford the vaccine for large numbers of people. Some countries, however couldn't afford large amounts of vaccine. Also, the vaccine was unstable—it wouldn't last if stored too long. It quickly lost its potency if it got too hot. Because of this, the vaccine wasn't easily transported to tropical climates.

In 1947, there was an outbreak of smallpox in New York City. This spurred the development of a more stable vaccine. Within a few years, the vaccine was made more stable by freeze-drying it, so it could be stored for months, even in hot climates.

In 1947, an outbreak of smallpox occurred in New York City. To stop the disease, thousands of New Yorkers lined up at city hospitals, health stations, city police stations, and at the Department of Health for free vaccinations.

In 1958, the World Health Organization (WHO) took on a global strategy against smallpox. In 1966, there was an international agreement to wipe out smallpox within 10 years. At that time, there were still 10 to 15 million annual cases of smallpox occurring in 44 countries. Whenever there was an outbreak, WHO doctors rushed in and aggressively vaccinated the community. Sometimes the progress of vaccination was slowed by wars. Sometimes the surveillance and communication systems failed. But the WHO continued its aggressive efforts. Better technology helped the process. Vaccination "guns" were invented that could vaccinate people much faster. When a case of smallpox appeared, doctors rushed in and found all the people who had contact with the victim. All of those contacts were then vaccinated. Next, they found all the contacts of those contacts, and vaccinated them also. Called "ring vaccination," this technique was a very effective way to quickly stop the spread of the dreaded disease.

The smallpox virus.

Ali Maow Maalin, of Merka Town, Somalia, had the world's last recorded case of smallpox. He survived, and no further natural cases of smallpox have occurred.

By 1975, smallpox only occurred in a small area of Africa, in the region of Ethiopia and Somalia. The area was experiencing civil war, and refugees were scattering in all directions, so vaccination was difficult. Still, the WHO continued to wage the smallpox battle.

Finally, the last naturally occurring case of smallpox occurred in 1977, in a man in Merka Town, Somalia. Hundreds of his contacts were vaccinated, and the contacts of their contacts were vaccinated. The man survived, and no other case occurred. Since then, there have been no more natural cases of smallpox.

However, smallpox was to cause one last tragic situation. In England in 1978, a smallpox virus escaped from a lab and infected a young woman. Officials tracked down 341 people who may have had contact with her, and revaccinated all of them. The disease also spread to the young woman's mother. The director of the laboratory, who already had been warned about the unsafe conditions and careless procedures of the lab, took his own life. The mother survived, but the young woman died. She was the last person ever to die of smallpox.

In December 1979, a global commission stated that smallpox had been eradicated. In 1980, the World Health Organization accepted the findings and officially declared that smallpox was dead and gone.

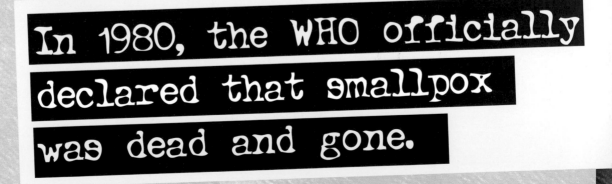

In 1980, the WHO officially declared that smallpox was dead and gone.

DESTROY IT OR STUDY IT?

After the laboratory deaths in England in 1978, it was easy for the World Health Organization to convince nations to destroy their remaining laboratory smallpox stockpiles. Remaining stockpiles were submitted to a steam pressure cooker, effectively destroying one of the greatest killers in the history of the world.

The WHO suggested that two stockpiles not be destroyed—those at the Centers for Disease Control in Atlanta, Georgia, and the Research Institute for Viral Preparations in the city of Moscow in the Soviet Union.

One by one, countries stopped the vaccinations of their populations. They stopped vaccinating their soldiers and their doctors. It looked like the world would never have to worry about smallpox again. But then, there were some disturbing developments.

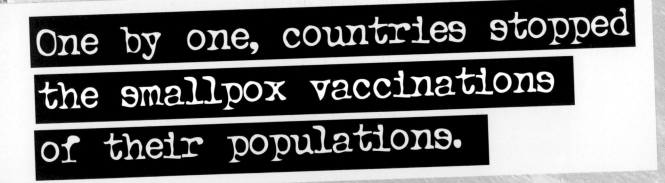

One by one, countries stopped the smallpox vaccinations of their populations.

A Maryland facility prepares to manufacture the smallpox vaccine. Though the disease is eradicated, fears of bio-weapon attacks are causing the United States to renew its supplies of the vaccine.

In 1991, the Soviet Union disintegrated into 15 separate countries. During the chaos and confusion as the government of the Soviet Union fell, it's not clear what happened at the laboratory that held the smallpox stockpiles. Some say that some of the scientists got jobs in other countries. Some of the stockpiles may have been moved.

Then, in 1992, a Soviet official came to the United States, defecting from his home country. He described a program in which the Soviets worked to turn smallpox into a military weapon. How much of what he said was true? Intelligence analysts still debate that question. Defectors are notorious for making exaggerated claims.

On September 11, 2001, terrorists made a horrific attack on American soil. Immediately, government official began to worry about other kinds of attacks. Smallpox was one of their first concerns.

Could a smallpox vial have been stolen in 1991 from Moscow, and could a terrorist group use it as a weapon? It's a theoretical possibility. But it would take a huge amount of know-how, and very specialized knowledge, to weaponize smallpox. Also, why make a weapon out of something that can be easily vaccinated against?

Still, after September 11, 2001, the U.S. government ordered millions of units of smallpox vaccine, and began to vaccinate soldiers and medical personnel.

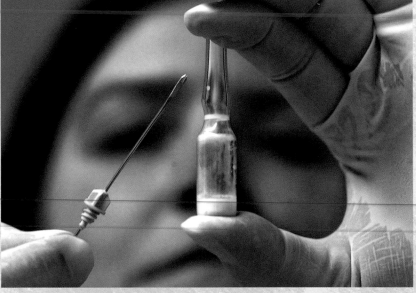

A medical worker holds a special bifurcated (two-pronged) needle and serum for 200 doses of smallpox vaccine.

What should be the fate of the remaining stockpiles of smallpox? The debate in the medical community still rages. Some people say the stockpiles should be destroyed. This would prevent any accidental escape, such as what happened in 1978. Other people say that scientists should keep the stockpiles, in order to study the genetic makeup of the virus, and understand it better.

So far, smallpox, the greatest killer in the world, has escaped execution.

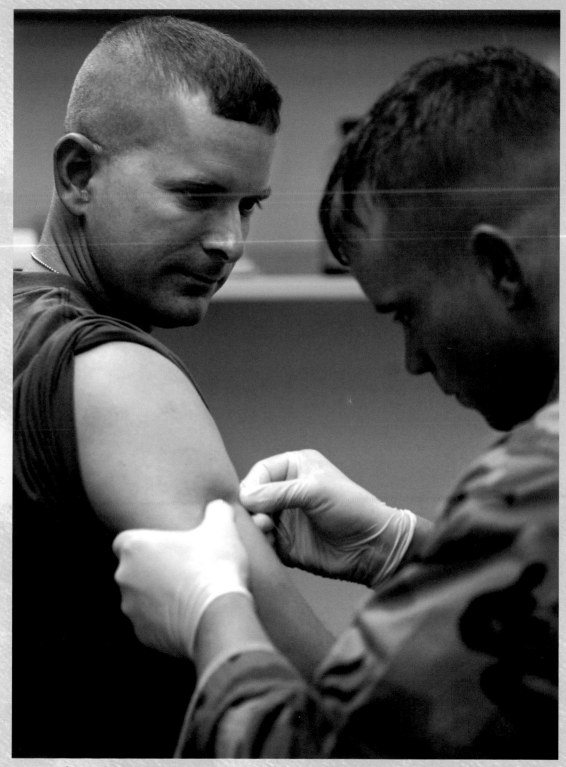

A United States marine receives a smallpox vaccination.

GLOSSARY

DNA

DNA is short for the scientific term Deoxyribonucleic Acid. In living things, DNA is the material inside the center of every cell that forms genes. This material is inherited from an individual's parents.

EPIDEMIC

When a particular disease spreads across a wide region. Smallpox was very contagious and could easily be caught by those nearby.

ERADICATE

To kill off completely. The smallpox germ has officially been considered eradicated in the natural world since 1980.

VACCINATION

The process of giving a person a dead or weakened form of a germ (vaccine), so that the immune system will recognize it and give the person an immunity to the germ. Edward Jenner gave people a cowpox virus, which was similar enough to smallpox that it gave people immunity to smallpox.

VARIOLA MAJOR

The scientific name for a version of the smallpox virus that is much more deadly.

In 1980, three former directors of the Global Smallpox Eradication Program read the good news that smallpox is dead.

Variola minor

The scientific name for a version of the smallpox virus that is less deadly than *Variola major*.

Variolation

The practice of inserting a small amount of smallpox fluid into a cut in a healthy person. This usually gave the person a mild case of smallpox. It was fatal about 3 percent of the time. Variolation fell into disuse when Edward Jenner developed the smallpox vaccination with cowpox.

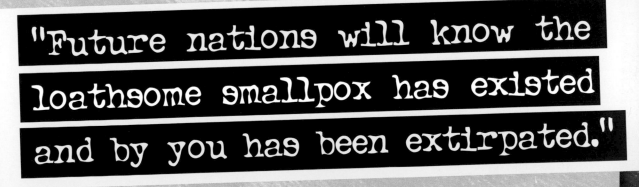

"Future nations will know the loathsome smallpox has existed and by you has been extirpated."

—President Thomas Jefferson, 1806, in a letter to Edward Jenner

INDEX